First World War
and Army of Occupation
War Diary
France, Belgium and Germany

1 DIVISION
Divisional Troops
75 Field Company Royal Engineers
1 April 1919 - 23 September 1919

WO95/1254/2

The Naval & Military Press Ltd
www.nmarchive.com
Published in association with The National Archives

Published by

The Naval & Military Press Ltd

Unit 10 Ridgewood Industrial Park,

Uckfield, East Sussex,

TN22 5QE England

Tel: +44 (0) 1825 749494

www.naval-military-press.com

www.nmarchive.com

This diary has been reprinted in facsimile from the original. Any imperfections are inevitably reproduced and the quality may fall short of modern type and cartographic standards.

© **Crown Copyright**
Images reproduced by permission of The National Archives, London, England, 2015.

Contents

Document type	Place/Title	Date From	Date To
Heading	WO95/1254/2		
Heading	1 Div Troops (Western Div) 75 Fld Coy RE Previously will Gds Div 1919 Apr to 1919 Sept		
Heading	B.E.F. France & Flanders 1 Division. Troops. 409 Fd Coy Royal Engineers (Formerly 1/1 Lowland) 1917 Feb To 1919 Sept. 75 Field Coy. R.E. 1919 Apr To 1919 Sept. (Formerly With Guards Div 76 Field Coy R.E. 1919 Apr To 1919 Aug. (Formerly with Guards Div)		
Heading	75th Field Co R.E. War Diary For April 1919		
War Diary	Tripplesdorf Germany	01/04/1919	05/05/1919
War Diary	Munstereifel Germany	06/05/1919	31/07/1919
Miscellaneous	C.R.E. Headquarters. Reference your C49 M. 2-9-19	02/09/1919	02/09/1919
War Diary	Munstereifel Germany	01/08/1919	10/08/1919
War Diary	Merten Germany	11/08/1919	26/08/1919
War Diary	Kinmel Park Camp N. Wales	28/08/1919	31/08/1919
Heading	To Kinnel Park Camp H.Q.	25/09/1919	25/09/1919
War Diary	Kinmel Park Camp Rhyl N. Wales	01/09/1919	23/09/1919

WO95/1254/2

BEF

1 Div Troops
(Western Div)

---

75 Fld Coy RE
Previously with Gds Div

1919 Apr to 1919 Sept

B.E.F. FRANCE & FLANDERS
1 DIVISION.   TROOPS.
409 FD COY ROYAL ENGINEE[RS]
(FORMERLY 1/1 LOWLAND)
1917 FEB TO 1919 SEPT.
75 FIELD COY. R.E.
1919 APR TO 1919 SEPT.
(FORMERLY WITH GUARDS DI[V])
76 FIELD COY R.E.
1919 APR TO 1919 AUG.
(FORMERLY HITH GUARDS DI[V])

1254

B.E.F. FRANCE & FLANDERS.
1 DIVISION. TROOPS.
409 FD COY ROYAL ENGINEERS
(FORMERLY 1/1 LOWLAND)
1917 FEB TO 1919 SEPT.
75 FIELD COY. R.E.
1919 APR TO 1919 SEPT.
(FORMERLY WITH GUARDS DIV)
76 FIELD COY R.E.
1919 APR TO 1919 AUG.
(FORMERLY HITH GUARDS DIV)

75TH FIELD Co R.E.

WAR DIARY FOR APRIL 1919.

Army Form C. 2118.

WAR DIARY
or
INTELLIGENCE SUMMARY.
(Erase heading not required.)

Instructions regarding War Diaries and Intelligence Summaries are contained in F. S. Regs., Part II. and the Staff Manual respectively. Title pages will be prepared in manuscript.

Place	Date	Hour	Summary of Events and Information	Remarks and references to Appendices
TRIPPELSDORF GERMANY	April 1st	–	"Julin" awaiting 3rd Bn. MUNSTEREIFEL. 1 Julin awaiting 3rd Bn. ARLOFF. NS was shop staff clean. Camp sulia improvements. 40 OR joined unit	
	2nd		20 OR joined from 421 R.E. GR. 20 OR Denabilises	
	3rd		1 OR 1/4/19	
	4th		2 OR 7/4/19	
	5th		1 OR 1/4/19. 50 OR Denabilises	
	6th		Voluntary Church Parade. 50 OR joined from 105 Field GR. 30 OR Denab. 1 OR Enrolls Res	
	7th		"Julin" area GY 2nd Bn. MUNSTEREIFEL. 1 No Julin ARLOFF. 6 OR joined from 23 Field.	
			Keum shop staff elena. Camp improvements. Drill.	
	8th 7/4/19			
	9th 7/4/19 – 30 OR Bombs. 40 OR of Fields. 2 OR 156 Field R.E.			
	10th 7/4/19 50 OR joined from 152 Field R.E. 40 OR 153 Field.			
	11th 7/4/19 120 OR Denabilises			
	12th 7/4/19 6 OR Denabilises			
	13th 7/4/19 30 OR Denabilises . 1 OR transferred 276" Field R.E.			
			Church Parade. New.	
	14th 7/4/19 –			
	15th 7/4/19			
	16th 7/4/19 – 70 OR Denabilises			
	17th 7/4/19 26 OR Denab 8c.			
	18th		Good Friday. general sliving forms. Voluntary Church service. 180 OR transd	
	9th 7/4/19			
	20th		20 OR Denabilises . Voluntary Church Parade.	
	21st 7/4/19			

Army Form C. 2118.

WAR DIARY
or
INTELLIGENCE SUMMARY.
(Erase heading not required.)

Instructions regarding War Diaries and Intelligence Summaries are contained in F. S. Regs., Part II. and the Staff Manual respectively. Title pages will be prepared in manuscript.

Place	Date	Hour	Summary of Events and Information	Remarks and references to Appendices
TRIPPELSDORF GERMANY.	22"		Italian advancing to the MUNSTEREIFEL – 1 Italian army in billet AKLOFF A.E. Workshops staff and cars. Company are billeted COMMERCIA.	
	23"		on 22/4/19. 10R. Divisione – Regimental Working Arrangements.	
	24"			
	25"		on 22/4/19 –	
	26"		on 22/4/19 – 20R Transfer BRS. Dept. Cotham	
	27"		on 27/4/19	
	28		on 27/4/19 Church Parade.	
	29		on 27/4/19	
	30		on 22/4/19 – 10 OR working u –	
			Changes and Supply during Month April 1st – 30th 99.	
			Arrivals. 40 OR	Evacuations Sparline etc.
				Sick. 2 OR
				Transfers. 3 OR
				Own Unit Sick – 97 OR.
			Strength of Company	
			1/4/19 8 Officers 261 OR	
			30/4/19 7 Officers 175 OR.	

[signature]
Major RE
O.C. 75 Field Coy RE

WAR DIARY or INTELLIGENCE SUMMARY

Army Form C. 2118.

Place	Date	Hour	Summary of Events and Information	Remarks and references to Appendices
TRIPPELSDORF, GERMANY	1/5/19	-	Weather unsettling but fair. MUNSTEREIFEL - Wilhelm ARLOFF - 2 Rating R.E. and shops	
	2/5/19		85th anniversary. Regiment carrying any activities are -	
	3/5/19		on 1/5/19	
	4/5/19		Church Parade. MUNSTEREIFEL, new rifle range. clearing movement.	
MUNSTEREIFEL, GERMANY	5/5/19		on 1/5/19. CHARLES Transferred to LANCASHIRE Div.	
	6/5/19		Command of unit transferred to Capt. a/Major T.G. Hyland, M.C. R.E.	
	7/5/19		Company moved to MUNSTEREIFEL, arriving 14 hour	
	8/5/19		W.D. commenced on 400 yd. Range. Drum trumpe.	
	9/5/19		2 Section Range. 1 Wilhelm ARLOFF, 1 Camp Duties	
	10/5/19		Lt. S. Major R.P. Wilshin attached to Denstbijkton. 1 O.R. admitted to hospital.	
	11/5/19		Lt. R.A. James attached on leave to U.K.	
	12/5/19		Voluntary Church Parade. 2 O.R. evacuated C.C.S.	
	13/5/19		W.D. commenced on Conversion of German Rifle Rays. MUNSTEREIFEL.	
	14/5/19		1 O.R. wounded. G.C.S.	
	15/5/19		3 Sections 400 yd. Range / ARLOFF & German Range.	
	16/5/19		2 O.R. transferred to W.D. Coy.	
	17/5/19		2 O.R. identified & 2 O.R. transferred from 76"Coy & 409 Coy. R.E. respectively	
	18/5/19		3 Section 400 yd. any. 1 Wilhelm ARLOFF & German Range, 4 PAdmns trported to hospital	
	19/5/19		Voluntary Church Parade	
	20/5/19		3 Section 400 yd Range, 1 ARLOFF & German Range	
	21/5/19		Same as 19 C.	

WAR DIARY
INTELLIGENCE SUMMARY

Army Form C. 2118.

Place	Date	Hour	Summary of Events and Information	Remarks and references to Appendices
MUNSTEREIFEL	22/5/19		2 O.R. demobilized	
GERMANY	23/5/19		3 Sections 400 yd. Range. 1 Sec. German Range. Workshops &c.	
	24/5/19		Company Workshops. Transferred from ARLOFF to IVERSHEIM.	
	25/5/19		2/Lt. R. Bates R.E. proceeded to join F.V.K. Voluntary Church Parade.	
	26/5/19		3 Sections 400 yd. Range. 1 Sec. German Range & Workshops &c.	
	27/5/19		T/F.E.J. Toy R.E. proceeds on leave E.V.K. 2/Lt. J.H.T. Fox proceeds on leave upon attachment from 26 Field Coy R.E. 2/Lt. P.A. James returned from leave & proceeded to Rastatum to TRIPPELSDORF	
	28/5/19		2/Lt. G. Kirwa returned to Coy from TRIPPELSDORF. 3 Sections 400 yd. Range. 1 Sec. German Range - Workshops &c.	
	29/5/19	2230am	Sapt 6 217401 Shr. Colleran E.V. (aged 32 years) at 37 C.C.S. COLOGNE from Pulmonary Tuberculosis. Command of Unit transferred to Capt. G.B.P. Bull. M.C. R.E. Capt. & Major F.G. Hyland transferred to War Office.	
	31/5/19		Charge in Strength during month 1/5/19 - 31/5/19. Departure 25. Arrivals 28.	
			Strength of Company: 1/5/19 - 9 Off + 150 O.R. 31/5/19 - 9 " + 158 "	

G.B.P. Bull
Capt. R.E.
O.C. 75 Field Coy. R.E.

WAR DIARY
INTELLIGENCE SUMMARY

Army Form C. 2118.

78TH FIELD COMPANY
30 JUN 1919
ROYAL ENGINEERS

HQ WESTERN DIVISIONAL ENGINEERS
A.440

Place	Date	Hour	Summary of Events and Information	Remarks and references to Appendices
MUNSTEREIFEL GERMANY.	June 1		2/Lieut. 1/Cpl. 9/N.C.O.'s. 172 O.R. & 37 attached. 13 O.R. W.S.A. transferred to this Company & 1 O.F. Capt. G. Hogan F.E. Hyland left for Cdn. of Cadet at dunkirk on the war Office. Typist from Western.	
	2.		2 Section 400 × Rays. 1 Section German Rays & 1 Sect. Workshops. RE. Recreation Hut. MUNSTEREIFEL	
	3.		2. O.R. transferred to Company from 409 Field Co RE. the following promotions were effected 42192 A/Sjt. Boham W. to L/Cpl A/Sgt to Cpl. A/Sgt Kerr, Nibblay, Whelley.	
	4.		42192 A/Sgt. Day. A.L. to C/Sgt	
	5.		9. O.R. proceeded on Demobilization	
	6.		1. O.R. admitted to hospital	
	7.		1. O.R. admitted to hospital	
			2. Section 400 × Rays. 1 Section German Rays 1 Section Workshops ×	
	8.		Voluntary Church parade	
	9.		2 Section 400 Rays. 1 Section German Rays. 1 Section Workshops. German Labour to 2 Recreation Huts.	
	10.		4 Offr. 7 N.C.Os proceeded on leave to U.K. Orders for 53 F.W.O. Completed	
	11.		1. O.R. admitted to hospital & 1 O.R. reported from hospital. Strength 8 Offs. 163 O.R. & 37 attached	
	12.		C.E. 2nd Army inspected Company. Work on 400 × Rays & German Rays.	
	13.		1. O.R. admitted to hospital	
	14.		A/Sgt Burns. G. proceeded to BONN in the course. Rg N°. 49033 Sapper Cotton L.E. died 8. conf'd. 11/6/16. awarded Military Medal, London Gazette 11-2-19. Rate Completed	
	15.		Voluntary Church parade.	
	16.		2 Section 400 × Rays. 2 Section Workshops. Recreation Hut ××. Reg. N°. 25462. Dross Quick. received Orders Imperial at MUNSTEREIFEL by Coy Let out with his electric works	

Army Form C. 2118.

WAR DIARY
or
INTELLIGENCE SUMMARY.
(Erase heading not required.)

Instructions regarding War Diaries and Intelligence Summaries are contained in F.S. Regs., Part II. and the Staff Manual respectively. Title pages will be prepared in manuscript.

78TH FIELD COMPANY, ROYAL ENGINEERS — 30 JUN 1919

H.Q. WESTERN DIVISIONAL ENGINEERS

Place	Date	Hour	Summary of Events and Information	Remarks and references to Appendices
MUNSTEREIFEL GERMANY.	June 17.1919		Orders for next march — all work stopped at mid day.	
	18.		Company marched to OBERDREES. Gd. Buck died of his injuries.	
	19.		Company marched to TRIPPELSDORF arriving at 10.30 hours — took up its billets.	
	20.		Church Parade at EUSKIRCHEN until full military honors. Company provide party. Military party under Lieut. R. Brown.	
	21.		Company Parade 08.00 hours. Drill Order. Rifle & B.R. Inspection. Compulsory Church Parade in Roestem Schule at 11.00 hours.	
	22.		D. Lieut. FEA visit 13.0.R. Attached to EISENBORN CAMP for work on Artillery Rage.	
	23.		Company Parade 8.00 hours. Drill Order. Rifle & B.R. Inspection. 2 motor cycles arrived from D.E.H.Q. 5 O.R. Party were transferred on Strike the 29's Infantry Bt.	Voluntary R.C. Service at BORNHEIM
	24.		Company Parade 8.00 hours. 2 Drivers transferred from 76 Field Co. R.E. 5 O.R. Attached to EISENBORN CAMP with 3rd Cav. Brigade, Officer's Charge	
	25.		" " " B.R. Inspection & Drill. B. Lieut. G. Thomas rejoined from leave.	
	26.		Company Parade 8.00 hours. B.R. Inspection & Drill.	
	27.		" " Drill Order. Route March to LECHTEM.	
	28.		Guard awarded to 2nd Lt. S. Smith by Captain who had rifled Mrs Otto Wacker in a travel. Two civilians attempt to break into officers mess at night.	
	29.		Cor Filgut 240.R. Attached EHERTON — Further Water Supply scheme being proceeded in search.	
	30.		Company Parade 8.00 hours. Departure Strength of Company 1/6/19 Officers 11 O.R. 170 30/6/19 " 8 " 165	
				1W.O. 270.R. Arrivals 20 O.R.

G.H.M. Matthews Capt. R.E.
O.C. 78 Field Co. R.E.

Army Form C. 2118.

75 Field Co. R.E.

WAR DIARY
or
INTELLIGENCE SUMMARY.

Month ending July 31. 1919

(Erase heading not required.)

Instructions regarding War Diaries and Intelligence Summaries are contained in F.S. Regs., Part II. and the Staff Manual respectively. Title pages will be prepared in manuscript.

Place	Date	Hour	Summary of Events and Information	Remarks and references to Appendices
MUNSTEREIFEL GERMANY	1/7/19		Company Parade 8.00 a.m. Gas Inspection & Drill. 1 Sarjt & 1 Company Offr & 16 S.O.R.	
	2/7/19		Company returned to MUNSTEREIFEL & resumed normal station. Transport by road & thence by train.	
	3/7/19		Work recommenced in Range MAHLBERG CAMP.	
	4/7/19		Peace celebration day. Company worked in 400th Regt.	
	5/7/19		MAHLBERG CAMP cancelled. Section (No 3) returned to H.Q.	
	6/7/19		Voluntary Church Parade.	
	7/7/19		Company Parade 8.00 a.m. Work in Range Workshops. Batt 116 to MUNSTEREIFEL & IVERSHEIM.	
	8/7/19		Offr Charge signed on 2/7/19 evacuated to M.O.S. now definitely struck off strength.	
	9/7/19		1 O.R. reported from Hospital & 1 O.R. admitted to same.	
	10/7/19		Brigade Whistley to celebrate Peace. 550 R. went to Rhine Trip.	
	11/7/19		100R returned to 400th Regt. 1 O.R. admitted to Hospital - reported by a mule.	
	12/7/19		Military Cross awarded to Lieut R. Brown of the unit.	
	13/7/19		Brigade Church Parade. IVERSHEIM.	
	14/7/19		Work in 400th Regt. 1 Motor Bicycle arrived.	
	15/7/19		1 O.R. reported to demobly schm.	
	16/7/19		400th YH. Regt. MUNSTEREIFEL Completed.	
	17/7/19		Work commenced at ARLOFF, MUNSTEREIFEL & IVERSHEIM.	
	18/7/19		Company Lottery & reception of work in Range. 1 Offr & 120 O.R. reported from Detachmt at ELLENBORN.	
	19/7/19		Voluntary Church Parade. Cricket match & afternoon v. D.E.H.Q. at Rodesberg. 1 Offr & 120 O.R. went to D.E.H.Q. 49 mm. D.E.H. 68 St.	
	20/7/19		Company Parade 8.00 a.m. New work commenced. 11 O.R. Infantry transferred to unit.	
	21/7/19		Work at ARLOFF, MUNSTEREIFEL & IVERSHEIM. 400th Regt Canst. commenced.	
	22/7/19			

P.T.O

Army Form C. 2118.

75 Fd Coy C.R.E

WAR DIARY
or
INTELLIGENCE SUMMARY.

(Erase heading not required.)

Month touching 31 July 1919.
(continued)

Instructions regarding War Diaries and Intelligence Summaries are contained in F. S. Regs., Part II. and the Staff Manual respectively. Title pages will be prepared in manuscript.

Place	Date	Hour	Summary of Events and Information	Remarks and references to Appendices
MUNITEREIFEL	24/7/19		No 2 Section with T.H. Honda proceeded to ALFTER. Fr work with 2nd Brigade Area.	
GERMANY.	25/7/19		WM.L. ARLOFF, MUNITEREIFEL. also pioneer field grounds, 3rd Brigade.	
	26/7/19		All parades cancelled. 3rd Bde Sports IVERHEIM. Company competed unsuccessfully in L.D Race.	
			Company 3rd L. Ople Jumping Competition. L 1st L Wrestling on Mule.	
	27/7/19		T.K. J.H.S Fox transferred to 409 Field Coy. & T.H G. Honda to 567 A.T. Coy.	
			Voluntary Church Service	
	28/7/19		Company Parade 7-30 A.M. Work at ARLOFF, MUNITEREIFEL, IVERTHEIM & 400 X Range Camp	
	29/7/19		Major W.H. Beachy, D.S.O. R.E. arrived & took over command of Company.	
	30/7/19		Company Parade 7-30 A.M. Work at ARLOFF & IVERTHEIM. Completed.	
	31/7/19		Work on 400 Yd Range Camp. MUNITEREIFEL, & Camp Improvements.	

Strength of Company 1/7/19 8 officers — 165 O.R.
"   "   "   31/7/19 7 "   — 176 O.R.

G.O.P. Nield Capt R.E.

For O/c 75 Field Co. R.E.

C.R.E.
Headquarters.

75th FIELD COMPANY,
ROYAL ENGINEERS.
No. R.20.
Date 2-9-19.

Reference your C.49 d/ 2-9-19.

Herewith completed War Diary for month of August.

All duplicates have been despatched to R.E. Records, Chatham, please.

H.Q. WESTERN
DIVISIONAL
ENGINEERS.
C.49.

G.W.P. Nettles
Capt. R.E.
A/ O.C. 75 Field Co. R.E.

75 Field C.R.E.　　Month ending Aug. 26. 1919.

Army Form C. 2118.

WAR DIARY
or
INTELLIGENCE SUMMARY.
(Erase heading not required.)

Instructions regarding War Diaries and Intelligence Summaries are contained in F. S. Regs., Part II. and the Staff Manual respectively. Title pages will be prepared in manuscript.

Place	Date	Hour	Summary of Events and Information	Remarks and references to Appendices
MUNSTEREIFEL GERMANY 1919.	Aug 1		Strength of Company. 7 Officers. 183 O.R. Work to 400th Royy. Camp. + Capt. Drake washing + fatiguing transport &c.	
	2.		Company Parade 8.00 hours. Rifle - Kit Inspection. Work as above.	
	3.		Voluntary Church Parade.	
	4.		General Holiday.	
	5.		Company Parade 8.00 hours. Work to 400th Royy. Camp., Capt. Drake. Cookhouse IVERSHEIM &c.	
	6.		" " " " " " 400th Royy. Camp. Completed.	
	7.		" " " " " " Lieut R. BROWN. Left Company for transfer to 93 Field Co RE	
	8.		" " " " " " Left Company for cleaning transport &c.	
	9.		" " " " " " Whole Company for cleaning transport &c. 10.R. admitted to hospital + 1.OR returned from same. Cy Strength 6 Off + 172 O.R	
	10.		Voluntary Church Parade	
MERTEN GERMANY	11		Company moved to MERTEN GERMANY	
	12		Company Parade 8.00 hours. Company equipment, horses &c overhauled + checked.	
	13		" " " " " Lieut P.A. JANES. transferred to 459 Field Coy. C.R.E.	
	14		" " " " " Checking of equipment Continued	
	15		" " " " " "	
	16		" " " " " Motor-Cycle accident at BRÜHL + admitted to hospital.		2nd Lieut E.J. TOY. R.E. injured +	admitted to hospital D.M.S. Coy ? RAMC
	17		Voluntary Church Parade. 2nd Lieut TOY. motor-cycle collided from Ireland D.M.S. Coy ? RAMC	

75 Field C.R.E.   Army Form C. 2118.

WAR DIARY
or
INTELLIGENCE SUMMARY.
(Erase heading not required.)

Month ending Aug. 26. 1919

Place	Date	Hour	Summary of Events and Information	Remarks and references to Appendices
MERTEN GERMANY	18.		Company Parade 8.00 a.m. Char Leon & Cleaning & checking of Equipment. Afternoon Abs. Parade & tk many of fatigue Cadre &c.	
	19.		Company Parade 8.00 a.m. With a view Entrained 40 O.R. departed & demobilised	
	20.		"	
	21.		"	Lieut W.A.P. WYNCH R.E - 6 O.R. departed
	22.		"Great Left" for ANTWERP with transport & equipment. Company Parade 8.00 a.m. Rifle Inspection & Kit Inspection. Lieut J. Enquiry with the Preliminary of Major Finlay V.C. D.S.O. M.C. R.E. held at BRÜHL to investigate the cause of accident to 2/Lieut E.J.T.O.E. R.E.	
	23.		Company Parade 8.00 a.m. 2/Lieut H.A.L. SHEWELL left for CALAIS with 40 O.R. Among the advance party of unit	
	24.		Company Paraded 10.30 hours & marched to ROISDORF then entrained for CALAIS.	
	25.		Company & train en route for Calais	
	26.		Company detrained CALAIS 17.30 hours & arrived for Rest at 10.30 hours. Company disembarked at 14 hours at DOVER & arrived at 9 hours for RHYL. N. WALES. Strength of Company 5 Off + 173 O.R.	
			Annual Grant R.H.L.	
			Strength of Company 1-8-19. 7 Off. 1130 O.R.
			26/8/19. 5 " 173 O.R.
			[signature] Major R.E.
			O.C. 75 Field C.R.E.

Army Form C. 2118.

WAR DIARY
or
INTELLIGENCE SUMMARY
(Erase heading not required)

75 Field Coy R.E.
Completion of Aug. 1919

Instructions regarding War Duties and Intelligence Summaries are contained in F. S. Regs., Part II and the Staff Manual respectively. Title pages will be prepared in manuscript.

Place	Date 1919 Aug.	Hour	Summary of Events and Information	Remarks and references to Appendices
KINMEL PARK CAMP N. WALES	28.		Strength of Company. 5 Officers + 168 OR. Company Parade. Clean fatigues 9.00 a.m. Gen. Duties. 20 K admitted to hospital	
	29.		Company Parade 9.00 a.m. Roll Call. Gen. Duties. Coal Fatigue + Kit Inspection	
	30.		" " " " " "	
	31.		Compulsory Church Parade 9.45 Kinmel. Major Ready D.A.O. proceeded on 7 days leave	
			Strength of Company 1/8/19 7 Off + 176 OR 5 - 164	
			" 31/8/19	

War Diary from 28-31st Aug. 1919
to complete

Major R.E.
OC 75 Field Coy RE

75th FIELD COMPANY,
ROYAL ENGINEERS

76th FIELD COMPANY
ROYAL ENGINEERS

R.11.
25/9/19.

To Kinmel Park Camp.
    H.Q.

Herewith Diary of this Unit to
complete month of August & also for
September up to 23rd inst. please.

G.M.Mills
Capt RE.

WAR DIARY or INTELLIGENCE SUMMARY.

Army Form C. 2118.

75 Field Company R.E.
September 1919

Place	Date 1919	Hour	Summary of Events and Information	Remarks and references to Appendices
KINMEL PARK CAMP. RHYL. N. WALES	1 Sept		Stay (?) of Company. 5 Officers. Drill Orders. Company Parade 9.00 hours. Kit Orderly. Capt. Durlie " Lieut. W.A.D. WYNCH Light fatigue. Lieut W.A.D. WYNCH promoted to Lieut.	
	2		Lieut. W.A.D. WYNCH promoted to Lieut. Company parade 9.00 hours. Clean fatigue. Capt. Durlie " 210.R. proceeded to demobilizatn. " Rifle Inspectn 14.00 hours	
	3		" " " " " " 8.O.R " 1 " " "	
	4		" " " " Drill ordr. Kit Inspectn. Capt. Durlie " 515247 Sapper Henshaw R promoted	
	5		" " " " Clean fatigue. Capt. Durlie " act/L/Cpl Sergeant.	
	6		" " " " Football Match I 6 Nethbury Cam Rt 75 R.E. 3. Athl 1.	
	7		Church Parade 9.45 hours	1.O.R proceeded to demobilizatn.
	8		Company 9.00 hours. Drill ordr. Rifle Inspectn Major W.H. Beardley D.S.O. R.E. resumed command of Company.	
	9		" " " " Clean fatigue. Kit Inspectn. Capt. Durlie " I.O.R. proceeded to demob	
	10		" " " " Kit order. Rifle Inspectn " " Capt. G.B.P. Brittle M.C.R.E proceeded to	
	11		" " " " Drill ordr. Rifle Inspectn " " Capt. G.B.P. Brittle M.C.R.E proceeded to 7 day leave.	
	12		" " " " Clean fatigue. Capt. Durlie " 40.O.R. proceeded to demobilizatn.	
	13		" " " " For Regmt march.	
	14		Church Parade 9.45 hours	Drill ordr. Capt. Durlie. For Regmt march.
	15		Stay (?) of Company. 5 Off + 170.O.R. Company parade 9.00 hours. 8.O.R. proceeded on demobilizatn. 66055 Sgt. Waterton J L/A acting A/C.S.M. Sgt. G.B.P. Brittle M.C.R.E 7 days leave (furlough) from Leave.	
	16		Company Parade 9.00 hrs. Rifle Inspectn Capt. Durlie 8.O.R. proceeded to demobilizatn. T.O.R.	
	17		" " " Clean fatigue. Capt. Durlie " 66055 Sgt. Waterton J L/A A/C.S.M. (acting) will	
	18		" " " " Kit Inspection Capt. Durlie effect from 12 cm inst.	
	19		" " " " Rifle Inspectn Capt. Durlie 15.O.R. proceeded to demobilizatn.	

P.T.O.

Army Form C. 2118.

75 Field Co. R.E.
September 1919
(Continued)

WAR DIARY
or
INTELLIGENCE SUMMARY.
(Erase heading not required.)

Place	Date 1919	Hour	Summary of Events and Information	Remarks and references to Appendices
KINMEL PARK CAMP. RHYL.	Sept. 20.		Company Parade 9.00 a.m. Clean fatigue. Bart. duties etc. Church Parade 9.45 a.m.	
	22		24 O.R. (Dismounted) proceeded to NEWARK + 15 O.R. (Mounted) proceeded to ALDERSHOT DEPOT.	
	23		Remainder of Company 4 Officers + 10 R (Details Codes) awaiting orders as to disposal at Kinmel Park Camp. RHYL. N.WALES.	

[signature]
Major R.E.
O.C. 75 Field Co. R.E.

75th FIELD COMPANY,
ROYAL ENGINEERS.
No.
Date.

www.ingramcontent.com/pod-product-compliance
Lightning Source LLC
Chambersburg PA
CBHW081508160426
43193CB00014B/2618